Inspiring Leaders

NATIVE AMERICAN HEROES

BY DAWN QUIGLEY

Consultant: PATRICIA JOLLIE
Enrolled Member of the Confederated Salish and Kootenai Tribes
Museum Research and Scholarship,
National Museum of the American Indian

SCHOLASTIC INC.

What are Native American Tribes?

There are more than 570 Native American **tribes**, or **nations**, in the United States. Each nation is **sovereign**, which means that each tribe has the right to govern and make decisions about its land and Native people. An **enrolled member of a tribe** is determined by each nation and may be based on a historical role or document to show citizenship. An **elder** is a respected member of a tribe who has lived a full life. Elders often tell us stories to teach important life lessons.

Native American or **American Indian** are terms that are sometimes used interchangeably. However, it is also important to use the specific tribe. For example, the author of this book is a tribally enrolled member of the Turtle Mountain Band of Ojibwe (ND). An **Indigenous** person comes from a certain land or area. A Native American is indigenous to the land of their tribal ancestors. The term Indigenous always connects a Native people to a certain land.

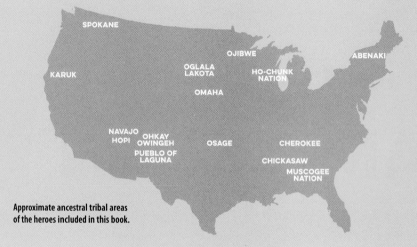

Approximate ancestral tribal areas of the heroes included in this book.

To all of the heroes out there, especially the unknown ones who guide our every day.

ISBN 978-1-338-56566-9
14 13 12 11   21 22 23
Printed in the U.S.A.   40
First printing 2019

Book produced by 22 MEDIAWORKS, INC.
lary@22MediaWorks.com
President LARY ROSENBLATT
Design and Production FABIA WARGIN DESIGN
Writer DAWN QUIGLEY
Editor SUSAN ELKIN
Copy Editor LAURIE LIEB
Photo Researcher DAVID PAUL PRODUCTIONS

PHOTOS ©: cover top left: Photographer © Nancy Bundt 2017; cover top right: Photograph by Jason S. Ordaz, Institute of American Indian Arts; cover bottom left: PA Images/Alamy Stock Photo; cover bottom right: NASA; 2: Yelena Jumelya/Shutterstock; 3: Jack Mitchell/Getty Images; 4: Courtesy Penguin Random House LLC; 5: Michael Greenlar/The Image Works; 6: Army Photo/U.S. Department of Defense; 7: Jack Kurtz/Zuma Press; 8: Cover of The Sioux Chef's Indigenous Kitchen by Sean Sherman with Beth Dooley. Published by the University of Minnesota Press, 2017. Used by permission; 9: Amy Forliti/AP Images; 10: Photograph by Jason S. Ordaz, Institute of American Indian Arts; 11: Harry Hamburg/AP Images; 12, 13: NASA; 14: Timothy A. Clary/Getty Images; 15: LM Otero/AP Images; 16, 17: Courtesy Whitney Baird; 18: Courtesy The Ross Family; 19: © 2019 United States Mint. All Rights Reserved. Used with permission; 20: Alpha Historica/Alamy Stock Photo; 21: Bob Nichols/USDA; 22: Hulton-Deutsch Collection/Getty Images; 23: Courtesy Columbia-Artists; 24: North Wind Picture Archives; 25: Library of Congress; 26, 27: Mark Davidson/Alamy Stock Photo; 28: Dennis Cook/AP Images; 29: Peter Turnley/Getty Images; 30 top: Jane Johnston Schoolcraft, HS4906, Johnston Family Papers, Bentley Historical Library, University of Michigan; 30 bottom left: Charlie Riedel/AP Images; 30 bottom right: Juan Labreche/AP Images; 31 top: Sam Bond; 31 bottom: Architect of the Capitol; 32: Tadpole Photography.

Maria Tallchief (Osage)

INTRODUCTION

What is a hero? Is it someone who makes a lot of money or who is famous?
No. A Native American hero is someone who uses her or his abilities and talents to
help fellow Native people and non-Native people live better lives. Native American
heroes are role models who encourage others to respect one another, and who
inspire us to learn about Native American history, language, and culture.

In this book you'll read about all kinds of Native American heroes, what their
childhoods were like, what they studied, and why we celebrate them.

This book features only some of our Native American heroes. But remember, a
hero doesn't have to be famous or well-known. A hero can be a parent who helps
you learn to read, a sibling who shows you how to bead, an uncle who cheers you
on at your sporting events, an elder who models how to support Native American
communities. Maybe someday, others might call *you* a hero. ■

JOSEPH

Have you ever read or heard a great story?

One that makes you laugh or cry, or makes you want to hear more? Joseph Bruchac, from the Abenaki Nation, is a Native American author who has written hundreds of books, plays, and short stories. He has won many awards for his work.

Joseph was born on October 16, 1942, in Greenfield Center, New York. He was raised by his grandparents. His grandfather, a member of the Abenaki tribe, left school at a young age because of racism. Yet Joseph wanted to learn about his Native American heritage. He loved to listen to the Native elders in his community tell stories about their people. Joseph's grandmother also loved to read and kept their house filled with books. But at that time it was hard to find written stories about Native Americans for him to enjoy.

Joseph went to Cornell University in the 1960s and studied literature and creative writing. He wanted to write stories that featured Native characters. Yet, at that time, there were no support systems in place at his school for Native students. Once again, Joseph turned to the elders for help. He learned more about storytelling and Native culture by visiting local reservations, asking questions, and listening.

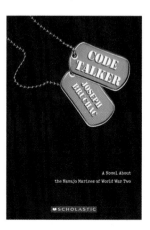

Today, Joseph's work is inspired by these stories. He makes sure his readers know where, or what tribe, his story is from. And he makes sure that the stories he is telling are something a Native nation would want to be told.

Joseph has dedicated his life to sharing, creating, and telling Native American stories, for example his acclaimed novel *Code Talker*. He has won many awards for his work. ▪

BRUCHAC

Joseph plays many Native American instruments, including the hand drum and wooden flutes.

After her death, Lori was awarded many military honors, including the Purple Heart for being injured in combat and the Prisoner of War medal. She was also given a promotion to the rank of specialist following her death.

LORI PIESTEWA

(1979-2003)

Have you ever had a friend who helped keep you safe?

In many situations, heroes are the people who protect us. Lori Piestewa, from the Hopi Nation, served in the US Army from 2001 to 2003. She was killed during the war in Iraq when the road she was traveling on was hit by bombs. Lori was the first Native American woman to be killed in combat. She was also the first woman in the US military killed in the Iraq War.

Lori was born on the Navajo Indian Reservation in Tuba City, Arizona, on December 14, 1979.

Lori joined the army after graduating from high school. She served in the 507th Maintenance Company, a support and maintenance team. On March 23, 2003, while driving through an Iraqi desert in a convoy, her group ran into an enemy ambush. Wanting to keep her fellow soldiers safe, Lori tried to drive away from the danger quickly. A rocket-powered grenade hit her Humvee. She and the others were taken prisoner. Sadly, Lori died from her injuries before they were released. Some of the people she served with shared the story of Lori's courage.

Native warriors have always protected our land, even before the founding of the United States of America. Native Americans always have lived here and always will. Soldiers and veterans are respected and revered by their Native American community.

In 2003, the Native American Games were renamed the Lori Piestewa National Native American Games. In 2008, Lori Piestewa was recognized for her extraordinary bravery in protecting her fellow soldiers. A mountaintop in Arizona was named Piestewa Peak in her honor. ■

Native American veterans of the US military honor Lori Piestewa's memory with a gourd dance, a ceremony performed on reservations in Oklahoma to honor returning soldiers.

SOLDIER (HOPI)

SEAN

Do you like to cook? Sean Sherman is a Native American chef who studied Indigenous foods. His catering business combines his love of cooking with respect for the wisdom of the elders, as well as for animals, plants, and the elements of nature. Sean is on a mission to show how food can connect Native people to our culture, families, and history. As owner of The Sioux Chef catering company in Minnesota, Sean wants all of us to understand the healthy way we used to eat, and how to make the most of our foods now.

Sean was born in 1974 on the Pine Ridge Reservation in South Dakota. He and his little sister grew up on their grandparents' ranch and went to elementary school in Batesland, South Dakota, where the Lakota language was taught during the school day. Sean, his sister, and cousins spent their free time outdoors exploring the land. By the time he was seven years old Sean knew how to use a rifle. He would hunt and gather foods such as chokecherries and wild turnips.

Sean also spent time with his family attending powwows, parades, Sun Dances, naming ceremonies, and more. Many traditional foods were served at these gatherings. Most of the food came from the land.

When Sean was older he moved to Spearfish, South Dakota. He took a job at a resort and soon began to cook there, experimenting with food such as beaver and rattlesnake. He learned about local plants that can be used for both food and medicines. In his early twenties, he moved to Minneapolis, Minnesota, and continued to work in restaurants.

In 2014, Sean started The Sioux Chef catering company. Sean doesn't use many items found in big supermarkets. He cooks with seasonal food found locally in Minnesota and the Dakotas. He has written a cookbook and will soon open the Indigenous Food Lab in Minneapolis, where people can learn to cook in the Indigenous tradition. ■

SHERMAN

Sean Sherman is opening his own restaurant in Minneapolis featuring healthy Indigenous foods.

Charlene is a director of the National Coalition on Racism in Sports and the Media. She continues to teach people about the disrespectful practice of using Native American images as mascots.

CHARLENE

Does your school or favorite team have a mascot?

A mascot is a character that represents a team, group, or business. It usually is supposed to bring good luck and provide amusement for fans. Sadly, there are still teams that use Native American images as mascots. This is racist and wrong because Native Americans are not cartoon characters or made-up people. Charlene Teters is an activist who worked to change a university's mascot.

Charlene Teters was born in Spokane, Washington, on April 25, 1952, and is a Spokane tribal member. In 1989, she went to a basketball game at the University of Illinois, where she attended school. She observed a white student dressed as "Chief Illiniwek," a fictional Native American dressed in feathers and war paint. Chief Illiniwek was the university's mascot who would dance to a drumbeat for the crowd. Native drumming, dancing, and regalia, or dance outfits, are sacred and important to Native people. This mascot, a pretend Native leader, hurt and insulted Charlene and many others.

Charlene began to quietly protest outside sporting activities at the university. She carried a sign saying **INDIANS ARE HUMAN BEINGS**. This inspired other Native American university students who joined the movement to stop depicting Native people disrespectfully. A documentary called *In Whose Honor* followed Charlene's work. The film helped spread Charlene's message.

Charlene's mission includes teaching people that Native Americans did not just exist in the past. Seeing people dressed in outfits from hundreds of years ago makes them seem unreal. As Charlene says, "Native Americans are here, and we are contemporary people, yet we are very much informed and connected to our history."

TETERS

JOHN B.

Have you ever been the new kid in school? It can be hard. John B. Herrington was born September 14, 1958. He is a member of the Chickasaw Native American tribe. John moved fourteen times by the time he graduated from high school in Plano, Texas.

Like many children growing up, John wanted to be an astronaut, but didn't know how to become one. John did not know any astronauts or have someone to show him a way to reach his goal. But he loved shooting rockets with his brother and dad. John took his passion for space and, with hard work, made his dream a reality. Like his ancestors, John likes to solve problems when facing challenges. That quality helped him succeed in a difficult field.

John studied complex math and engineering in college. He went to the US Naval Test Pilot School in Maryland. A job at the National Aeronautics and Space Administration (NASA) in 1996 led to his dream of becoming an astronaut. On November 23, 2002, John became the first Native American in space on the shuttle STS-113 *Endeavour*.

Commander Herrington has logged, or been in space, more than 4,600 hours in many different types of aircraft. Honoring his Chickasaw heritage during his spacewalk, John carried a braid of sweetgrass, two arrowheads, the Chickasaw Nation flag, and six eagle feathers.

John encourages an Indigenous perception of space exploration, saying that Native ancestors have been observing nature and the sky for thousands of years. Today and yesterday, Native people have survived by studying their natural surroundings before the term STEM (science, technology, engineering, and mathematics) ever existed. ▪

John B. Herrington was the first tribally enrolled Native American to go to space, as well as the first Native American to walk in space.

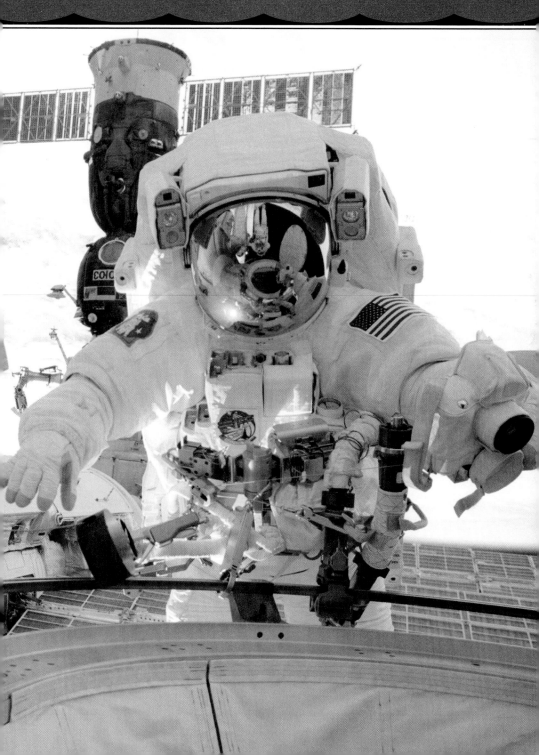

Have you ever ice-skated? Do you like to watch ice skaters compete on TV? Naomi Lang is an ice skater, and the first Native American woman to compete at a Winter Olympics.

Naomi Lang was born in California on December 18, 1978. She was inspired to begin ice-skating at the age of eight, after she saw a traveling skating show near her home. Naomi began taking lessons and soon combined her love of ballet with ice-skating to compete as an ice dancer. She and John Lee, her first skating partner, won the US Junior silver medal in 1996.

That same year, a Russian American man named Peter Tchernyshev saw Naomi skate at a competition. He liked her skating. He wrote to Naomi and asked if she would like to be his ice dancing partner. They met in New York to practice together and have been partners ever since. Naomi and Peter competed for the US in the 2002 Winter Olympic Games. They won many US ice dancing competitions. After retiring from professional sports, they traveled the world performing in ice shows, sometimes appearing on TV.

Naomi now teaches skating. Her students have gone on to participate in both Junior national and international competitions. Being a Native American athlete is something Naomi is proud of. She spent many hours training and wants to show other Native children that hard work pays off. She hopes to inspire others as a role model. ∎

During the 2002 Winter Olympic Games in Salt Lake City, Utah, Naomi and Peter earned three perfect presentation scores.

When you think of a Native American musician, who comes to mind? Gary Paul Davis, known as Litefoot, is from the Cherokee Nation. Gary is an actor, rapper, motivational speaker, author, and entrepreneur.

Gary was born September 11, 1968. When Gary was growing up in Tulsa, Oklahoma, he spent time working with his family in their auto shop and construction businesses. In his free time, he explored music. He loved hip-hop and Motown artists, along with traditional Native music, and began rapping under the name "Litefoot" in 1991. By watching his family work, Gary learned how to start his own business. He opened Red Vinyl Records in 1992 and became the first Native American rap musician. He worked hard, and with the support of his family and others, he became a success. He has since performed thousands of concerts and released eleven award-winning albums.

Litefoot wanted to make a difference in his Native community. He realized he could use his music to educate people about the issues his people face. Litefoot also saw too many non-Native musicians dressing up as Native American, in a disrespectful manner. It was important to him to help bring about positive change.

In 1994, Litefoot performed in Rome with the American Indian College Fund and sang contemporary, or modern, Native American music. After that he stayed busy performing all over the United States. Soon a film company contacted him to see if he wanted to

be in a movie. Since then, Litefoot has starred in numerous films and television programs. He has performed his music in many different countries. Everywhere he goes, he speaks out in support of Native issues around the globe. ■

Litefoot has won six Native American Music Awards including Artist and Album of the Year.

GARY PAUL

DAVIS

Mary helped
design plans for
satellites in orbit
and submarine-
launched vehicles.

MARY G. ROSS

(1908–2008)

Have you ever helped to solve a challenging problem?

Mary G. Ross was born August 9, 1908, in Park Hill, Oklahoma. Her great-great-grandfather, Chief John Ross, led the Cherokee Tribe on the Trail of Tears. This was an event in the 1830s when the US government forced tribes to walk many miles from their homelands to relocate in faraway Oklahoma. It led to death, relocation, and a loss of homelands and culture for many Native Americans.

As a teenager, Mary lived with her grandparents. She did well in school and enrolled in college to study mathematics when she was only sixteen years old. She also became interested in astronomy. After teaching for several years, Mary was hired as a mathematician at the Lockheed Corporation, where she helped design airplanes.

Mary excelled at her job, so the company sent her back to college to earn an engineering degree from the University of California. An engineer transforms complex ideas into working products or solutions. At that time, few women were studying or working in the engineering fields. Mary was the first known Native American woman engineer.

In 1952, Mary joined an ongoing secret project called Skunk Works, which explored space travel between planets. This was before any person had even traveled to space. She even created plans for space travel to Mars and Venus.

Mary Ross continued to be a Native American hero as she worked to encourage other young Native girls to become engineers. She won many awards for her work and even has a scholarship named after her. She was a member of the Society of Women Engineers and was active in the American Indians in Science and Engineering Society.

Mary grew up honoring the Cherokee value of learning. She has helped all of us see that even though it may be difficult to be the only one who looks like you in a job, you can do it. Even though it was challenging, Mary did it and showed us it can be done. ▪

The design for the 2019 Native American gold coin issued by the US Mint is a tribute to Native Americans in space. It depicts Mary G. Ross on one side.

NAVAJO CODE TALKERS

Corporal Henry Bake Jr. (left) and Private First Class George H. Kirk (right), serving with a Marine signal unit in the South Pacific during WWII.

Do you speak one language? What if you were a hero because of the language you spoke? One group of important Native American heroes are the Native soldiers who used their languages during World War II as a way to communicate and pass secret military messages in code.

Starting in the 1800s, the US government forcibly took Native children from their families and placed them in Native American boarding schools. This continued until the mid-1900s. The cruel policy separated families and robbed children of their Native culture. Yet the languages survived and are still passed down from each previous generation. Many Native people continue working hard to keep their language through efforts called Native American language revitalization. One of these languages, Navajo, was critical in aiding the US during WWII. Other Native languages including Comanche and Muscogee were also used for code talking.

In 1941, the US government began to recruit Navajo, or "Diné" as they prefer to be called, soldiers to develop a secret code based on their language. No other country could understand Navajo, which allowed our armed forces to send coded messages over the radio. Navajo soldiers on the receiving end would decipher the codes. Some examples of the coded messages included using the Navajo words for "metal fish," which meant "submarine," or the Navajo word "chicken hawk" for "dive bomber." Our enemies were never able to understand these messages.

Sadly, after the war the hero Code Talkers could not talk about the work they did because the US government kept their work secret from the public, or classified. In 1968, the world finally learned about the Navajo Code Talkers.

In 2001, the twenty-nine Navajo soldiers who created the codes were honored with the Congressional Gold Medal.

Many Native Americans served in the military during WWII. This land has always been our home, and Native heroes have, and still do, defend it with honor. Even though the government tried to stop Native children from speaking their tribal languages, our military leaders later realized the strength, wisdom, and knowledge contained in these Native languages.

NAVAJO

Maria spoke out against Native American stereotypes and prejudiced ideas about Native Americans many times.

MARIA TALLCHIEF

(1925–2013)

Have you ever been the first to do something? Maria Tallchief, from the Osage tribe, was America's first major prima ballerina, or top dancer, in a ballet company. Maria was also the first Native American to hold this title.

Elizabeth "Betty Marie" Tallchief was born on January 24, 1925, in Fairfax, Oklahoma. When she was three years old she began to take dance and piano lessons. A few years later the family moved to California so she and her sister could continue training as dancers. Betty Marie moved to New York City when she was seventeen years old. She hoped to earn a place with a large ballet company. She changed her first name to Maria. Some ballet teachers suggested she also change her last name to something sounding more European, but Maria refused. Tallchief was her name and she was proud of it.

She joined the Ballet Russe de Monte Carlo, a touring ballet company based in New York City, where she spent the next five years. There, she met a famous choreographer, or person who creates and plans the dancers' movements, named George Balanchine. In 1946, when Balanchine helped to start what is now called the New York City Ballet company, Maria was its first celebrated dancer.

In the New York City Ballet, and later in Paris, other dancers did not want to recognize how truly great Maria's dancing was. They would not give that kind of praise to a Native American. But soon the other dancers and audiences realized that Maria was a truly gifted ballerina. She became the first American to dance with the Paris Opera Ballet.

Maria became known as one of the world's greatest dancers and held the title of prima ballerina for eighteen years. After retiring, Maria moved to Chicago to start the Lyric Opera's ballet school and Chicago City Ballet.

In 1999, she was presented with a National Medal of the Arts by the National Endowment for the Arts. It is one of the highest honors an artist can receive. ■

PRIMA BALLERINA (OSAGE)

Think you could create your own written language?

How would you do it? In 1821, a man from the Cherokee Nation created a written form of the Cherokee language. This is called "syllabary," and it is a kind of alphabet. Native American languages have always been, and still are, oral, or spoken aloud. Sequoyah's syllabary transformed the oral Cherokee language so it could be read and written down.

Sequoyah was born in Tuskegee, a Cherokee town in what is now Tennessee. He had problems with one of his legs from birth, or perhaps from an accident early in life, but this did not stop him. Sequoyah became a skilled tradesperson, and then later a silversmith.

In the early 1800s, as newcomers settled around them, Natives began to share ideas about settler people's way of writing. Sequoyah understood that the written marks actually stood for sounds that could be understood as words. He wondered if he could do the same thing for the Cherokee language. He believed he could transform the oral sounds into a written form as a way to help his people. Some teased him for this idea, but again this did not stop Sequoyah.

Creating this new written form was challenging. Sequoyah first included many symbols for each word of the Cherokee language, but that became overwhelming. On his next attempt, he listened carefully to the sound chunks that made up words. He created 86 characters, or symbols—one for each sound of the Cherokee oral language.

At first, no Cherokee adult would learn Sequoyah's new syllabary. But he would not give up, so he taught his daughter. Soon he was able to show how this new written form of communication worked. After many demonstrations, the western Cherokee accepted it. The eastern Cherokee were also persuaded to learn the new system and awarded Sequoyah a silver medal to honor him. ■

Sequoyah became a leader in his tribe and represented his people in negotiations with the US government. Many things, animals, and places are named after him, including mountains, a county, giant trees in California, a caterpillar, and numerous schools.

SEQUOYAH
(c. 1770–1843)

CHERI MADSEN

Cheri Madsen became the first Native American woman to win a bronze medal in an Olympic exhibition event.

Have you ever finished a goal, but then decided to take it up again much later?

Cheri Madsen, from the Omaha tribe, is an American Paralympic athlete who races in a wheelchair. She won many races and medals in her twenties, but when she had children, she retired from the sport. Or at least she thought she did.

The Paralympics is an international sporting event with thousands of athletes competing from more than one hundred countries. These athletes are physically disabled and face a variety of challenges.

Cheri was born on September 27, 1976, in Omaha, Nebraska. When she was three years old she woke up one day and found herself unable to walk. An unknown virus caused Cheri's leg paralysis.

When she was a teenager, Cheri began wheelchair racing. At her first meet she qualified for the Junior national competition. Cheri kept racing and getting stronger and faster. Two years later, she made the US Paralympic team. She competed in the 1996 and 2000 Paralympics and won many medals. A documentary was made about Cheri's accomplishments.

After the 2000 Games, when she was twenty-four years old, she retired from sports because she wanted to have children and raise a family. She and her husband have two daughters.

Cheri's younger brother, Mario, kept asking her when she was going to start training again for wheelchair racing. Cheri was surprised he would ask this because she had retired. Yet Mario always encouraged Cheri to get back into sports. Sadly, in 2007, both Mario and their father were killed in a car accident. This tragedy led to Cheri's decision to come out of retirement.

After much hard work and training, today Cheri Madsen is back racing and winning more medals than ever.

What does the leader of a nation look like or sound like?

What does it take to become a leader? Wilma Mankiller became the first female elected Principal Chief of the Cherokee Nation.

Wilma Mankiller was born in Tahlequah, Oklahoma, on November 18, 1945. When she was eleven years old her family moved to California. Wilma shed many tears about having to move away from her homeland.

As she grew older and attended college, Wilma began spending time with the San Francisco Indian Center. In 1969, some Native Americans took control of and occupied an abandoned prison called Alcatraz, in San Francisco Bay. They did this to protest how the US government was failing to uphold Indian people's rights. Wilma was inspired and became passionate about advocating for Native people.

Wilma moved back to Oklahoma in the 1970s to work for the Cherokee Nation's government. She supported her Native community in various projects. A serious car accident in 1979, and a neuromuscular disease, left Wilma with a long recovery. She had a lot of time to think about how she wanted to live her life. She knew she wanted to be of service to her people for a long time to come.

Wilma overcame her health challenges and, in 1983, was elected the Deputy Chief of the Cherokee Nation. She took over as the Principal Chief in 1985. She was the first female to serve in that position. Wilma remained Principal Chief until 1995.

In 1998, President Bill Clinton awarded Wilma the Presidential Medal of Freedom for all of her work.

Wilma helped the tribe grow by making health care more available, improving schools, providing job training, and more. She continued to teach, give speeches, and write about how to advocate and support Native people until she died.

A leader does not come in one color, gender, or ability. Wilma Mankiller did not give up, but instead overcame challenges to lead and help her people. ▪

WILMA PEARL MANKILLER

(1945–2010)

JANE JOHNSTON SCHOOLCRAFT
WRITER AND TRANSLATOR

Jane Johnston Schoolcraft (1800–1842) was born in what is now Michigan. She was a talented writer. Bamewawagezhikaquay, Jane's Ojibwe name, means "Woman of the Sound That Stars Make Rushing through the Sky." She was the first known female Native writer and the first to write down poems in her Native language. Jane could speak both Ojibwe and English. She was the first known Native author to listen to Indian people tell traditional stories and then translate and transcribe them into English.

SHARICE DAVIDS AND DEB HAALAND
CONGRESSWOMEN

In 2018, the first two Native American women were elected to the US Congress: Representatives Deb Haaland of New Mexico, member of the Pueblo of Laguna, and Sharice Davids of Kansas, member of the Ho-Chunk Nation. Also, Peggy Flanagan, of the White Earth Ojibwe, was elected in Minnesota as the state's first Native American lieutenant governor. In 2018, many other Native people were elected in other local positions. These Native heroes are shining the light, made possible by their ancestors, to guide us into the future.

CYNTHIA LEITICH SMITH
WRITER

Cynthia Leitich Smith, a citizen of Muscogee Nation, is a bestselling children's and young adult author. Cynthia earned a law degree before beginning her writing career. She has written sixteen books and many short stories. Cynthia also teaches college graduates how to write for children and young adults at Vermont College of Fine Arts. Not only is she an accomplished author and teacher, but Cynthia is also dedicated to supporting and mentoring new Native American writers to create a strong Native author community.

PO'PAY
(c. 1630–c. 1688) REVOLUTIONARY

Many people are familiar with the American Revolution that began in Massachusetts in 1775. However, there was another American Revolution many years before.

In 1680, after many years of oppression, a man named Po'pay led the Ohkay Owingeh people in a revolt against the Spanish so they could live in peace and freedom. Po'pay used a secret method of counting corded rope as a type of calendar so more than seventy Ohkay Owingeh communities would know when to rise up and fight together. Po'pay's revolt created Native independence for more than a decade.

TO LEARN MORE

To discover more about Native American history, culture, and/or language, check out your own state's tribal websites, the Native heroes in this book, or these online sources:

The National Museum of the American Indian:
americanindian.si.edu

American Indians in Children's Literature (AICL):
americanindiansinchildrensliterature.blogspot.com

ABOUT EACH HERO

josephbruchac.com

army.mil/americanindians/piestewa.html

sioux-chef.com

charleneteters.com/Charlene_Teters/Welcome.html

chickasawpress.com/Books/Mission-to-Space.aspx

nativepartnership.org/site/PageServer?pagename=aief_hist_nna_naomilang

litefoot.com/litefoot-biography

alltogether.swe.org/2018/08/remembering-mary-g-ross-first-american-indian-woman-engineer

americanindian.si.edu/nnavm/heroes

notablebiographies.com/St-Tr/Tallchief-Maria.html

webtest2.cherokee.org/About-The-Nation/History/Biographies/Sequoyah

teamusa.org/para-track-and-field/athletes/Cheri-Madsen

womenshistory.org/education-resources/biographies/wilma-mankiller

womenhistoryblog.com/2012/07/jane-johnston-schoolcraft.html

nytimes.com/2018/11/07/us/elections/native-americans-congress-haaland-davids.html

cynthialeitichsmith.com/about-cynthia/about-cynthia-leitich-smith

americanjourneys.org/aj-009b/summary/index.asp

ABOUT THE AUTHOR

Dawn Quigley, PhD and citizen of the Turtle Mountain Band of Ojibwe, ND, is an educator, author, and former Indian Education program director. She loves to read, write, and cook. Dawn lives in Minnesota with her family.